# D'Nealian® Home/School Activities:

## Cursive Practice for Grades 4-6

**Barbara Gregorich**

**Scott, Foresman and Company**
Glenview, Illinois    London

*D'Nealian® is a registered trademark of Donald N. Thurber,*

*licensed exclusively by Scott, Foresman and Company, and is used*

*here with permission. For a complete list of D'Nealian® products,*

*contact Scott, Foresman and Company, 1900 East Lake Avenue,*

*Glenview, IL 60025.*

For information about other Good Year Books®, please contact your local school supply store or

Good Year Books
Scott, Foresman and Company
1900 East Lake Avenue
Glenview, Illinois 60025

13 14 15 - MAL - 95 94 93

ISBN 0-673-18176-6

# Contents

# Teaching Handwriting:
## A Conversation with Donald N. Thurber
Author of Scott, Foresman D'Nealian™ Handwriting Program K-8

**Let's begin with a basic question. What is D'Nealian Handwriting?**
It's a program in which the inconsistencies and illogic of most traditional handwriting methods are eliminated. It involves a unique, lower-case manuscript alphabet that is very easy to write and that leads into cursive writing with virtually no trouble at all. Most letter forms are the basic forms of corresponding cursive letters. Also, most letters are formed with one continuous stroke so that rhythm, an essential ingredient in cursive writing, is built in from the beginning. The manuscript letters are slanted, as cursive letters are. As a result, when the time comes to learn cursive, the basic patterns are already there; the manuscript that has been learned is not unlearned but, rather, built upon. This saves a lot of teaching and learning time and effort.

Another aspect of D'Nealian Handwriting is that it does not require use of oversize primary pencils and large writing lines at the early stages. Some young children may do better with very large pencils, but not all. So I recommend that teachers make writing instruments of various sizes and fairly small writing-line size available to children from the very beginning. Flexibility is what's important. For example, a teacher who wants to use unlined or large-line paper for beginning practice can.

**How does D'Nealian handle legibility?**
One of the most important points about the program is that it stresses legibility but recognizes the fact that writing is an individual product and that no two people write alike. One child's writing may be larger than another's; one may slant to the right while another slants to the left; one may make more circular parts while others may make more oval shapes. If teachers look for consistent slant, size, and spacing in children's writing, legibility will develop. The main thing to remember is that writing is an individual skill endeavor.

**Yet, the D'Nealian program does have model letters—with a certain slant—for children to imitate, does suggest writing-line sizes, and does recommend a certain spacing. What makes D'Nealian Handwriting more individualistic than other programs?**

Models are given because children need *something* to start with. For example, I recommend a "normal" slant (about fifteen to twenty degrees right slant) based on study of thousands of children's papers. The point is that D'Nealian doesn't insist that all children follow someone else's slant precisely. So long as they're consistent, students can write vertically, slant to the right, or slant to the left. Look for legibility, period. That's why the program does not include any kind of transparent overlays for children to place over their own writing for evaluation purposes. That's simply against the D'Nealian philosophy.

Children entering school are highly motivated to learn to write, and this method builds on that motivation by treating handwriting as the individual effort that it is. Children compete against themselves, trying to improve their own legibility, rather than compete against an artificial standard. Children are happier and do better work in this kind of learning situation. D'Nealian does not frustrate them by demanding the impossible. The result is what I hear over and over again from teachers using the method: "The pupils *like* to write now." That's very refreshing. . . .

**Did you ever encounter a teacher or teachers who liked the method but felt unable to use it while the rest of the school or district used another method?**
In fact, I've heard only good things from teachers. They like D'Nealian because it saves them time—they don't have to teach two totally different methods of writing, manuscript and cursive. Teachers also like it because the pupils like it and do well with it; they achieve greater legibility at an earlier age and move smoothly into cursive writing. *That's very satisfying for teachers, parents, and children.* . . .

**When and how does a teacher actually go about teaching D'Nealian Handwriting?**
Some handwriting teaching can be done in kindergarten. But I would not want to set a goal that all children should write the manuscript alphabet by the end of kindergarten. Most children don't start to do a decent job with handwriting until around the middle of first grade. So, formal handwriting teaching probably should begin in first grade.

As for the actual teaching, start with lower-case manuscript *a* and drill. And let me emphasize *drill* for that one particular letter until children have got the concept of the stroke movements. For early practice, children can use their finger to "write" the letter in the air, on the desk, in the palm of their hand, or in sand; they can trace it on a chalky chalkboard; the teacher can write the letter on the board, and they can erase it with their finger; they can write it on the chalkboard themselves. When the kids are ready to start actually writing on paper, I think they should get into free-hand writing right away, with little or no writing over models. Writing over models is not really relevant to the philosophy of D'Nealian Handwriting. Besides, it gets boring for students after a while.

After *a*, the other lower-case manuscript letters are introduced in such a way that one skill is built upon another. By introducing letters in a certain pattern, words can be written early. I want children to write words quickly. By teaching words in practice writing, rather than isolated letters, you begin teaching the concept of left-to-right, an important aspect of beginning reading. Also, you are building basic vocabulary words.

**Are letters taught in alphabetical order?**
No. Letters are taught according to similarity of formation. Alphabetical order is important, but who says when it has to be learned? With D'Nealian Handwriting, children learn a couple of vowels and a couple of consonants almost right away. They can make some words, some phrases. As they learn more letters, they make more words. After they've learned how to make all the letters, alphabetical order will come. . . .

**When is cursive taught?**
There is no one right time for all children to begin cursive. But by the middle of second grade, the average child probably is ready for it. Of course, if the pupils have had D'Nealian Handwriting from kindergarten on, there may be quite a few who have already moved to cursive on their own. I've seen that in classrooms. Those children who aren't ready for cursive by the end of first grade should stay with manuscript until it is mastered.

With D'Nealian, transition is so easy. Most manuscript letters become cursive letters with the addition of simple joining strokes. As with manuscript, all lower-case cursive letters are taught and mastered before capitals are introduced. Lower-case and capital cursive letters are taught in an order according to similarity of formation, though the important new things are really the joining strokes, not the letters themselves.

Practice should continue to be meaningful. For example, the daily handwriting period could open with kids writing an experience story, even if it's only a sentence in response to a question like, "What did you do yesterday after school?" . . .

**Earlier, you talked about meaningful practice in the form of words, phrases, sentences, and stories. What else can teachers do to make handwriting meaningful to students?**
Well, there are so many possibilities for application activities. They can range from composing get-well notes in the primary grades to answering job advertisements in the upper grades. Especially in the middle and upper grades, handwriting materials have to be highly motivational. The students are getting pretty sophisticated about some things, and a lot of repetition or drill isn't going to do anything for them. Teachers can make use of the special interests of their students to develop meaningful handwriting activities. For children who desire or might have artistic ability, calligraphy would be a good study. . . .

**Do children who learn D'Nealian Handwriting have any special problems reading the other kinds of letter forms they encounter elsewhere?**
No more trouble than students who learn other handwriting methods. Most books, for example, use print that isn't anything like any kind of handwriting—circles-and-sticks or D'Nealian. So it really doesn't make any difference. Even so, in the Scott, Foresman D'Nealian™ Handwriting program, especially in the first-grade book, kids are shown how the various letters look in book print. . . .

**What role can parents play in teaching handwriting?**
Most parents are very eager for their child to learn, to achieve. I would say to parents: Don't push; don't try to do too much formalized teaching. But it just makes sense that the earlier the school lets parents know what it is doing with handwriting, the more likely it is that kids will come to school writing in a fashion something like D'Nealian Handwriting.

In Gibralter [Michigan], we have a spring kindergarten roundup, when parents bring their child to see the school. At this time, we've been giving parents copies of the D'Nealian lower-case manuscript alphabet along with the directions for forming the letters. We don't encourage the parents to teach the entire alphabet, by any means. We do ask that if they want to work on handwriting at home they try to follow the method that will be used in school the next year. In D'Nealian Handwriting books for readiness and first and second grades, letters to families, with the D'Nealian letters and numbers printed on the back, serve the same kind of purpose.

# To The Teacher

Concerned only with cursive handwriting, not with manuscript handwriting activities, *D'Nealian™ Home/School Activities* is meant to serve as a supplement and enrichment activity book for teachers and parents who want to provide extra cursive handwriting activities for young students.

## Purpose
The main purpose of the book is to provide specific exercises for extra handwriting activities. Because the D'Nealian method treats handwriting as a communications tool, however, and not merely as a mechanical skill, the activities in the book emphasize handwriting as communications. For example, students might be asked to write a poster for a garage sale; they might be asked to write a greeting card to send to a friend; they might be asked to exchange their riddles, radio advertisements, or other written activities with a fellow student, each reading the other's writing.

Communication skills involve not only having something to say (as in the examples above) but also being able to think something through before saying it. Therefore, teachers who give young students the activities in this book will be helping to improve the students' ability to think and communicate clearly. The same activities that provide beneficial practice in handwriting skills also provide important exercise in thinking and writing skills.

## Student Level
This book is designed with the average fourth and fifth grade student in mind. Some activities may be suitable for advanced third graders who are learning cursive writing; other activities might be suitable for sixth-grade writing assignments. There is no reason why a third and sixth grader should not write on the same subject matter. They simply will bring different interests and skills to the writing activity.

## Organization
*D'Nealian™ Home/School Activities* consists of four sections:

1. lower-case D'Nealian™ letters
2. upper-case D'Nealian™ letters
3. D'Nealian™ arabic numerals
4. supplementary materials

Although the sequence of activities corresponds to the order in which D'Nealian™ letters are taught in school, the teacher may use the pages in any order that is appropriate. Activities in any one section are not dependent upon the activities in another section.

Each page contains at least four activities, usually organized from the simple to the more complex. Three symbols are used throughout the book to indicate three specific categories of handwriting activities.

This symbol indicates that the activity is basically concerned with the writing of single words. For example, the student may be asked to write a list of ten words, each word beginning with the letter "y." Or the activity may require changing a given group of ten words into ten different words by changing only one letter per word, and so on.

This symbol indicates that the activity is basically concerned with the writing of single sentences. For example, the student may be asked to write a series of five sentences, each beginning with a **w word**. Or the activity may involve making a greeting card with a one-sentence greeting/comment, and so on.

This symbol indicates that the activity is basically concerned with the writing of longer exercises, such as single- or multiple-paragraph compositions. Activities involving the writing of small stories, reports, advertisements, and so forth carry this symbol.

## Supplementary Materials

Portions of a conversation with Donald N. Thurber—creator of the D'Nealian™ Handwriting System—appear on pages iv and v. His remarks will refresh the teacher's memory as to the purpose and reasoning behind D'Nealian™ handwriting. At the back of the book, on pages 35-40, are various illustrations to reproduce for specific writing activities.

## Using the Book

Here are several suggestions for the teacher using this book.

- You—the teacher—will be the person using *D'Nealian Home/School Activities*. The young student will not see the pages of this book, except for the illustrations which you may duplicate. As a result, you will need to write some of the words on a sheet of paper or on the chalkboard, or you will have to read a list of words patiently to the student(s).

- Throughout this book, an expression such as **w word** or **b word** means simply a word that contains the letter "w" or the letter "b." A **w word** need not *begin* with "w," but it must *contain* a "w."

- Some students may strongly prefer single-word activities to paragraph compositions. Since the main purpose of this book is to improve handwriting skills, give individual students the activities they enjoy most. On the other hand, do not ignore a student's particular needs; a youngster may need practice in the longer writing assignments. Try to strike a balance between what the student prefers and what she/he needs.

- Avoid giving several handwriting activities at one time. In most cases, one activity—or, at most, two—a day will be enough to give the student sufficient handwriting and thinking/writing practice.

- Whenever you think it is appropriate to do so, ask students to exchange papers and read each other's handwriting activities. Reading other people's handwriting helps convey the idea that handwriting is a means of communication.

From *D'Nealian™ Home/School Activities: Cursive Practice for Grades 4–6*, published by Scott, Foresman and Company. Copyright © 1985 Barbara Gregorich.

# To The Parent

If you have purchased this book in order to provide your child with additional cursive handwriting activities at home, be certain to read "To The Teacher" on pages vi and vii. It explains the content and organization of *D'Nealian™ Home/School Activities*.

After you read "To The Teacher," read the suggestions below. You may find that one or more of them are quite relevant to you and your child.

- **Writing Style.** The D'Nealian™ method, unlike others, does not make children conform to a single slant of the paper, pencil grip, or slant of the letters. Therefore, allow your child to slant the paper and grip the pen or pencil in the way she/he is most comfortable. Likewise, do not insist that your child slant the letters in a particular direction. What matters is that your child writes letters that are *consistent* in their slant, not that they slant to the left or to the right.

- **Writing Materials.** Make sure that your child has four or five sheets of paper and two pencils or pens before beginning each activity. The child may use only one or two sheets, but children often feel more comfortable when they have extra paper on which they can doodle or take notes.

- **Your Handwriting.** Some of the activities require that you write a list or sentence for the child. Do not be concerned if you do not write in the D'Nealian™ style. Simply write in your own cursive script and allow the child to write in D'Nealian™.

- **Picture Activities.** *D'Nealian™ Home/School Activities* comes with illustrations (pages 35-40). Although these illustrations are intended for reproduction by the classroom teacher, you can have them duplicated on a photocopying machine. Since each illustration is used in at least two writing activities, make at least two copies of each of the six illustrations. A few extra copies might be advisable. Some children like to mark up or write on the photocopied illustration. Such marking or writing often helps the child organize his/her thoughts before writing, and you should encourage such behavior.

- **Reading the Handwriting.** If your child has a brother or sister of comparable age, you may ask them to exchange papers and read each other's writing aloud. If not, you might try reading the paper aloud. You might also try saving papers for a week and then asking your child to read them. Are they legible to the person who wrote them?

 Ask the student to label three columns across a sheet of paper. The columns should be labeled **old**, **all**, and **ill**. Then ask the student to make as many words as possible in each column by adding one or more letters to the word at the top. For example, in the column under **ill** the student might write *bill, chill, fill, pill, thrill, spill,* etc.

★ ★ ★ ★ ★ ★ ★ ★

 Ask the student to fold four standard sheets of unlined paper in half width-wise and then turn each sheet of folded paper so that it resembles a greeting card, with the fold on the left. On the front of each card, the student should write (in lower-case letters) one of these expressions—**last laugh**; **last but not least**; **lay down the law**; **leave well enough alone**— so that a different expression appears on each of the four cards. On the inside of each card, the student should write a greeting that uses the expression on the front. For example, *I love getting the last laugh. Ha!* Encourage the student to decorate the cards, and remind the student to use other **l words** in the sentences.

★ ★ ★ ★ ★ ★ ★ ★

 Ask the student to write titles for five computer games dealing with the following topics: a jungle adventure, a science fiction adventure, a mystery adventure, a western adventure, and a sports adventure. Each title must consist of at least two words, and at least one **l word** must appear in each title. For example, *The Tangled Jungle; Laser Blast;* etc.

★ ★ ★ ★ ★ ★ ★ ★

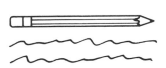 Ask the student to choose one of the computer game titles from the activity above and write an explanation of how the computer game will work. Afterwards, ask the student to underline all the **l words** in the explanation.

Ask the student to write the word *handwriting* across the top of a sheet of paper. Then, using only the letters in handwriting, the student should write as many smaller words as possible on the sheet. Each smaller word must contain the letter **h**. For example, *hat, thin, than, hid,* etc.

★ ★ ★ ★ ★ ★ ★ ★

Ask the student to construct two word triangles. The first triangle starts with the one-letter word **a** at the top and progresses to a five-letter word at the base by adding one letter to the word above. If necessary, the sequence of letters may be changed, but the second letter that the student adds must be **h**. For example:

a
ha
has
hats
hates

or

a
ah
ham
mash
shame

In the second triangle, the student must begin with an **i**, then add **h**, and progress one letter at a time to a five-letter word. For example:

i
hi
his
ship
ships

★ ★ ★ ★ ★ ★ ★ ★

Ask the student to write five questions about a school subject or subjects. The first word in each question must be one of the following—**who, what, when, where, why.** Encourage the student to use at least one other **h word** in each question.

★ ★ ★ ★ ★ ★ ★ ★

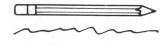

Ask the student to write about a field trip to the kitchen of a fast-food restaurant that serves **hamburgers, hot dogs, chicken,** and **fish.** The student must use each of these food **h words** at least once. In addition, he/she should use each of the following words at least once: **ketchup, hot mustard, relish, chocolate.**

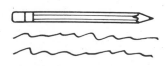

Ask the student to write a list of all the words pictured in Illustration #1 (page 35) that begin with the letter **k**. Encourage the student to use a dictionary to check the spelling of words of which she/he is uncertain. A score of 5 is good; 10 is outstanding.

★ ★ ★ ★ ★ ★ ★ ★

Ask the student to write **kn** and **sk** at the top of two columns on a sheet of paper. In the first column, the student should write as many words as he/she can think of that begin with **kn**. For example, *knee, kneel, knock, knife*, etc. In the second column, have the student write all the words she/he can think of that begin with **sk**. For example, *skin, skinny, skunk*, etc.

★ ★ ★ ★ ★ ★ ★ ★

Ask the student to write a series of funny sentences explaining any four of the following:

1. how the kangaroo got her pouch
2. how the monkey got its tail
3. why the elephant has tusks
4. why the koala has no tail
5. why the cricket chirps
6. how the elk got its horns
7. why the snake has no feet
8. why the stork has long legs

For example: *The koala has no tail because it was up a tree when tails were being handed out.*

★ ★ ★ ★ ★ ★ ★ ★

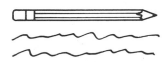

Ask the student to write a story about Illustration #1 (page 35). Encourage the student to use as many **k words** as possible in the story.

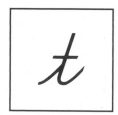

 Have the student write the following list on a sheet of paper:

1. a fish
2. a musical instrument
3. a sport
4. an animal
5. a bird
6. a vegetable

Then, next to each phrase, the student writes an appropriate word that begins with the letter **t**. For example, *a fish—* **tuna** or **trout**; *a musical instrument—* **trumpet**, **tuba**, or **trombone**.

★ ★ ★ ★ ★ ★ ★ ★

 Have the student make a list of at least five jobs or chores that he/she could do to earn money. Each entry in the list must have a **t word** in it (not counting the word "the"). For example: *babysit; cut the grass; empty the garbage;* etc.

★ ★ ★ ★ ★ ★ ★ ★

 Have the student write each of the following tongue twisters:

1. Ted threw Theresa thirty thumbtacks.
2. She stacked twelve thin sticks on three thick sticks.
3. Thin twin tooters tooted two flutes.

Ask the student to exchange papers with another student and say each tongue twister aloud. Then ask the student to make up a tongue twister that uses **t words**. You might want to supply the student with possible tongue-twisting **t words** such as **twin**, **this**, **thistle**, **thin**, **twice**, **twist**, **twine**, etc.

★ ★ ★ ★ ★ ★ ★ ★

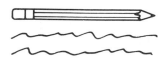 Ask the student to turn a standard sheet of unlined paper sideways and draw a mountain scene on it, creating a large postcard. On the reverse side of the postcard, the student should write a message to a friend or relative. The message should describe what the student sees on his/her trip, and it should include each of the following **t words** at least once: **mountain**, **earth**, **sight**, **tall**, **trees**, **flat**, **most**, **better**. Encourage the student to use as many other **t words** as possible in the postcard message.

From *D'Nealian™ Home/School Activities: Cursive Practice for Grades 4–6*, published by Scott, Foresman and Company. Copyright © 1985 Barbara Gregorich.

Ask the student to write and number as many words as he/she can think of that begin with the letter **i**. A list of 10 words is good, 15 excellent.

★ ★ ★ ★ ★ ★ ★ ★

Ask the student to number a sheet of paper from 1 to 10, then write each word pictured in Illustration #2 (page 36). For example, *1. mice*. Next to each word the student should write a rhyming word that contains the letter **i**. Here is what the first entry might look like:

> 1. mice      rice

★ ★ ★ ★ ★ ★ ★ ★

Ask the student to fold five sheets of standard unlined paper in half width-wise and turn the sheets so that they resemble greeting cards, with the fold on the left. Inside the five cards, the student should write one or more sentences expressing a greeting for each of the holidays listed below. The greetings must contain the **i words** that appear in the list below for the given holidays.

> 1. Holiday: Groundhog Day
>    **i words: winter** and **spring**
> 2. Holiday: Valentine's Day
>    **i words: valentine** and **friend**
> 3. Holiday: Fourth of July
>    **i words: picnic** and **invite**
> 4. Holiday: Halloween
>    **i words: which** and **witch**
> 5. Holiday: Thanksgiving Day
>    **i words: holiday** and **family**

For example: *Will we have spring or winter? Only the groundhog knows!* Either before or after the student has written the sentence, she/he might like to illustrate the front of the card.

★ ★ ★ ★ ★ ★ ★ ★

Ask the student to imagine being stranded on a tropical island with only a bottle of ink, a piece of paper, and a stick to write with. Have the student write a message to put in the bottle, using as many **i words** as possible in the message.

Ask the student to write a list of all the words beginning with the letter **u** pictured in Illustration #3 (page 37). Encourage the student to use a dictionary to check the spelling of words of which he/she is uncertain.

★ ★ ★ ★ ★ ★ ★ ★

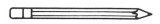

Have the student write the numbers from 1 to 10 in a column on a sheet of paper. Next to each number the student should write one of the following words: **happy, cover, able, fold, believable, lucky, fair, usual, tie, popular**. Then, next to each word, the student should write an antonym (word that means the opposite of the first word) by adding the prefix "un." For example:

    *1. happy    unhappy*

★ ★ ★ ★ ★ ★ ★ ★

Ask the student to write six sentences. Each sentence should contain one of the following words: **up, under, upon, until, about, quite**. Encourage the student to use as many **u words** as possible in each sentence. For example: *The rubber ball bounced up the stairs.*

★ ★ ★ ★ ★ ★ ★ ★

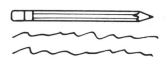

Ask the student to write a story about Illustration #3 (page 37), using as many **u words** as possible.

Have the student write the numbers from 1 to 5 on a sheet of paper and then write one of the following words next to each number: **elephant, elevator, eleven, earthquake, engine.** Next to each word, the student should write one or more smaller words that can be made out of the letters of the first word. For example:

*1. elephant       lap, tan, eel, heel, ant, pan, pen, hen*

★ ★ ★ ★ ★ ★ ★ ★

Ask the student to number a column on a sheet of paper from 11 to 20. The student should then write the word for that number next to each numeral. For example, *11. eleven.* Finally, ask the student to write a sentence for each number word, using as many other **e words** as possible in the sentence. For example:

*11. eleven*
*Eleven elephants weigh more than eleven tons.*

★ ★ ★ ★ ★ ★ ★ ★

Ask the student to write five sentences. Each sentence should contain one of the following words and one word that rhymes with it: **beep, neat, breeze, wreck, guess.** The student's rhyming word must contain an **e.** For example: *I did not beep the horn on the jeep.*

★ ★ ★ ★ ★ ★ ★ ★

Ask the student to write a story about the following situation. Seven icebergs are floating in the ocean, heading toward a passenger ship whose engines are broken. Can the ship be saved or the passengers rescued? After the student completes the story, ask her/him to underline all the **e words** in it.

Have the student write the numbers from 1 to 5 in a column on a sheet of paper. Next to each number the student should write one of the following words or phrases:

**short coat**
**denim pants**
**precious stones**
**run slowly**
**leap**

Then, on the same line, the student should write another word that the first word or phrase suggests. The student's word must begin with the letter **j**. For example, *short coat        jacket.*

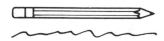

Ask the student to illustrate any three of the following: **jungle, jet plane, jam, juggler, jar, jellybeans**. After drawing the three pictures the student should label each one with the correct word, then write a sentence about each one using as many **j words** as possible. For example: *The jam is in a jar.*

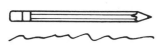

Have the student write each of the following words on a sheet of paper: **injure, rajah, major, unjust**. The student should then look up each word in the dictionary and write the definition next to the word. Finally, have the student write a sentence that uses the word.

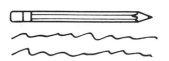

Have the student write the following words or phrases on a sheet of paper:

**in the jungle**
**hungry growl of the jaguar**
**jump**
**see its jaws open**
**just a movie**

Encourage the student to write a story using the phrases in sentences in a logical sequence.

Have the student write the numbers from 1 to 10 in a column on a sheet of paper. Next to each number the student should write one of the following words: **map, tan, dam, sand, nail, page, lake, shack, cramp, brass**. Ask the student to change each word into another word by changing only one letter—excluding the **a**, which must not be changed. The student should write the new word next to the given word. For example, *map    cap (or lap, nap, tap, rap, sap, man, mad, mat, etc).*

★ ★ ★ ★ ★ ★ ★ ★

Have the student turn a standard sheet of unlined paper sideways and write the words "Garage Sale" across the top. Then ask the student to list as many garage sale items as possible that contain the letter **a**. Encourage the student to illustrate the sheet so that it becomes an attractive poster for a garage sale.

★ ★ ★ ★ ★ ★ ★ ★

Have the student write a sentence for each pair of words:

**angry/alligator**
**airport/airplane**
**ants/army**
**absent/Andy**
**antelope/alert**

Each sentence must contain both words in the pair and should contain as many other **a words** as possible. For example: *An angry alligator ate my apple.* Encourage the student to write about any subjects in which he/she is interested: science, humor, fantasy, etc.

★ ★ ★ ★ ★ ★ ★ ★

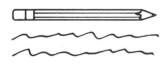

Ask the student to write a paragraph about space travel, using each of the following words at least once: **space, astronaut, spaceship, male, female, stars, Earth, blastoff**. Encourage the students to use the words in his/her own order.

Ask the student to number a sheet of paper from 1 to 12. Next to each number, the student should write the "ing" form of the verb pictured in Illustration #4 (page 38). Each verb must contain the letter **d**. For example:

1. *sliding*
2. *paddling*
3. *digging*

★ ★ ★ ★ ★ ★ ★ ★

Have the student write the following words on one sheet of paper: **dinosaur, daffodil, deer, daisy, dog, duck, dove, dogwood, dragonfly, dolphin, donkey, dormouse**. On another sheet the student should make two columns, labeling one "Plants" and the other "Animals." Ask the student to write each word from the list in the proper column. Encourage the student to look up any words he/she does not know.

★ ★ ★ ★ ★ ★ ★ ★

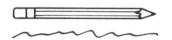
Ask the student to write five sentences in the following pattern:

*I am* _____ *when* _____ .

Each first blank should be filled with one of the following words: **glad, cold, loud, ready, sad**. The student should then complete the sentences by filling in each second blank. Encourage the student to use at least one other **d word** in each sentence. For example: *I am glad when I see ducks.*

★ ★ ★ ★ ★ ★ ★ ★

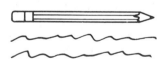
Ask the student to imagine lying in bed and hearing a dripping sound in the dark at midnight. Have the student describe the incident, including what is causing the sound and what the student does about it. Finally, ask the student to underline all the **d words** in his/her description.

From *D'Nealian™ Home/School Activities: Cursive Practice for Grades 4–6*, published by Scott, Foresman and Company. Copyright © 1985 Barbara Gregorich.

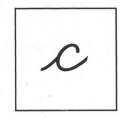

Ask the student to write a list of all the words she/he can think of pictured in Illustration #5 (page 39) that contain the letter **c**.

★ ★ ★ ★ ★ ★ ★ ★

Ask the student to write each of the following words on a sheet of paper: **moccasin, chocolate, magic, traffic, plastic, volcano, coconut, camera.** Then have the student look up each word in a dictionary and write a sentence that uses the word correctly.

★ ★ ★ ★ ★ ★ ★ ★

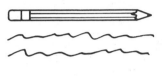

Ask the student to write a story about the scene in Illustration #5. Encourage the student to use as many **c words** as possible.

★ ★ ★ ★ ★ ★ ★ ★

Ask the student to write a radio commercial about a crispy snack made of corn and bacon chips that both city and country children love to eat. The commercial should describe the product and explain why children love to eat it. Remind the student to use as many **c words** as possible in the commercial. Finally, have students exchange papers and read each other's commercials as if they were making an actual radio announcement.

Ask the student to number a sheet from 1 to 5 in a column. The student should then write the following words in the numbered spaces: **you, plus, few, less, least**. Next to each word the student should write an antonym (word that means the opposite). Each antonym must begin with the letter **m**.

★ ★ ★ ★ ★ ★ ★ ★

Ask the student to write a sentence that contains as many words beginning with the letter **m** as possible. Encourage the student to write a funny or nonsense sentence. For example: *Merry Mark milks many mooing moose*. Students may exchange papers and read each other's sentences aloud.

★ ★ ★ ★ ★ ★ ★ ★

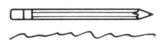

Ask the student to imagine that she/he is a scientist visiting the zoo. The scientist must write a description (one or more sentences) of each of the following animals' activities: **monkey, mule, mouse, camel, hummingbird**. Encourage the student to include as many **m words** as possible (in addition to the name of the animal) in each sentence that describes the animal's activities. For example: *The monkey moved quickly when it saw me.*

★ ★ ★ ★ ★ ★ ★ ★

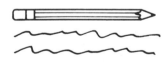

Ask the student to write a diary entry that tells what happened on a very stormy night. The student must use at least six of the following words at least once: **storm, room, home, dream, drum, tomorrow, somebody, family, chimney, lamp, jump**. Encourage the student to use the words in any order and to include as many other **m words** as possible in the diary entry.

Ask the student to write "ing" at the top of a sheet of paper. Below the heading, the student should write at least five words that end in "ing" and that have another **n** in them. For example, *ringing, singing, groaning,* etc.

★ ★ ★ ★ ★ ★ ★ ★

Ask the student to write five sports headlines. Each headline must contain at least two **n words**. For example: *Rangers Win Pennant!*

★ ★ ★ ★ ★ ★ ★ ★

Ask the student to make his/her own television viewing guide. The student should start by writing the words "Television Vision" at the top of a sheet of paper. Then she/he should list five program titles and write a description of that evening's episode. Each program title and each description must contain at least one **n word**. For example, *Wild, Wild World of Animals. The jungle life of a baboon is shown.* The program titles must be those of real TV shows, but the sentence descriptions may be invented.

★ ★ ★ ★ ★ ★ ★ ★

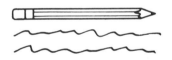

Ask the student to write a description of two astronauts, a man and a woman, landing on the moon. When the description is finished, the student should underline all the **n words** in the paragraph(s).

Ask the student to number a sheet of paper from 1 to 6. Next to each number, the student should write a one-word name of something he or she might like to be. For example, *ballplayer, astronaut, doctor*, etc. After the student completes the list, explain the meaning of the prefix "ex" (former; no longer as such; as in ex-President). Ask the student to add the prefix "ex" and a hypen at the beginning of each career name on her/his list. For example, *ex-ballplayer*.

★ ★ ★ ★ ★ ★ ★ ★

Ask the student to write three different sentences, each one using the words **fox** and **box** in it.

★ ★ ★ ★ ★ ★ ★ ★

Ask the student to write a list of at least five **x words**. Then ask the student to write five sentences, each one containing one of the **x words** and one of the following proper nouns: **Texas, Mexico, Maxine, Rex, Alexander**. For example: *My dad had to fix a flat tire in Texas.*

★ ★ ★ ★ ★ ★ ★ ★

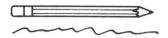

Ask the student to write about a band that has **sixty excellent saxophone** players and **sixteen extra xylophones** that need **fixing**. The student should use each of these **x words** at least once.

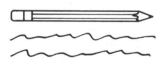

 Ask the student to write the following scrambled words in a column on a sheet of paper: **teg, ogt, asg, idg, urg**. Next to each scrambled word the student should write the word correctly. For example, *teg     get*.

★ ★ ★ ★ ★ ★ ★ ★

 Ask the student to label two columns on a sheet of paper, placing **gr** at the top of one column and **ight** at the top of the other. Beneath the first heading, have the student write the word **great**; beneath the second, the word **night**. Then ask the student to write as many other words as possible by adding one or more letters to the letters in the headings. For example, *green, greet, grow* for **gr**; *light, knight, bright, right* for **ight**.

★ ★ ★ ★ ★ ★ ★ ★

 Ask the student to write a sentence for each of the following words: **grass, igloo, giggle, green, grab, fudge, frogs, soggy**. Each sentence must contain one of the given words and a sense word (touch, feel, taste, smell, etc.). For example: *The fudge tasted sweet.*

★ ★ ★ ★ ★ ★ ★ ★

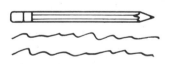
 Ask the student to write a funny story about a man who jogs in the fog. The humor in the story might come from a description of what happens to the man. Encourage the student to use as many **g words** as possible in the story.

Have the student write the following five words across the top of a sheet of paper: **flying, shy, crying, silly, furry**. Below each word the student should number a column from 1 to 5. Then, next to each number, the student should write a noun phrase using the adjective at the top of the column with a noun that is appropriate to one of the pictures in Illustration #1 (page 35). For example, **flying** kite, **shy** king, **furry** kittens. Finally, have the student write a complete sentence for each noun phrase. The student may not use the same noun more than twice in the five sentences.

★ ★ ★ ★ ★ ★ ★ ★

Have the student number a sheet of paper from 1 to 5. Next to the numbers, the student should write the following scrambled words: **oyu, tey, raye, dray, elly**. Then ask the student to unscramble each set of letters to form a word that begins with **y**. The student should write the correct word next to the scrambled one.

★ ★ ★ ★ ★ ★ ★ ★

Ask the student to write a poem that includes each of the following words at least once: **money, honey, sunny, funny**.

★ ★ ★ ★ ★ ★ ★ ★

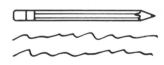

Ask the student to write a newspaper story about a **yellow yo-yo** contest in which **young players** must keep their **yellow yo-yos** moving while **saying** words that **rhyme**. Ask the student to use each of these **y words** at least once, and encourage him/her to use as many other **y words** as possible in the newspaper story.

From *D'Nealian™ Home/School Activities: Cursive Practice for Grades 4–6*, published by Scott, Foresman and Company. Copyright © 1985 Barbara Gregorich.

Ask the student to number a sheet of paper from 1 to 10, and then show her/him Illustration #6 (page 40). Have the student write the correct word for each picture next to the appropriate number on the sheet of paper. Although the correct words appear on Illustration #6, they are not matched to the pictures.

★ ★ ★ ★ ★ ★ ★ ★

Have the student write the following names on a sheet of paper: **Raquel, Monique, Dominique, Jacques, Enrique**. Then ask the student to think of and write at least five words that contain **q**. Finally, ask the student to write five sentences, each of which must contain one of the names and one of the other **q words**. For example: *Raquel squirted me with the garden hose.*

★ ★ ★ ★ ★ ★ ★ ★

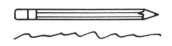

Show the student Illustration #6, and ask him/her to write five sentences using the words that name the ten pictures. Each sentence must contain two of the **q words** so that the student will use all ten of the given **q words** in the five sentences. For example: *A squid cannot swim in quicksand.*

★ ★ ★ ★ ★ ★ ★ ★

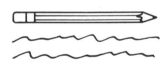

Ask the student to rewrite the story of the three little pigs and the big bad wolf. The new story will be about the three little squirts and the big bad squid. The little squirts can be young fish, lobsters, clams—whatever the student wishes to make them. Encourage the student to use as many **q words** as possible in the story. Here are some possibilities: **conquer, quiet, quick, question, squash, squish, squint, squeal, squeak, squeeze**.

Ask the student to write as many words as she/he can think of that end in the letter **p**. For example, *map, trap, pop, stop, trip, dip, dump, hump, cup, scoop, sleep,* etc. A list of 15 is good, 25 excellent, 35 outstanding.

★ ★ ★ ★ ★ ★ ★ ★

Ask the student to write each of the following words on a sheet of paper: **parrot, panda, potato, peach, peacock, porcupine, porpoise, pumpkin, peppermint, pelican, pepper, pear, poodle, pheasant**. Then have the student label two columns on another sheet of paper, placing the word "Animals" at the top of one column and the word "Plants" at the top of the other column. The student should categorize the **p words** above by writing each word in the appropriate column. For example,

| *Animals* | *Plants* |
|-----------|----------|
| parrot | potato |
| panda | peach |

Encourage the student to use a dictionary to learn about words he/she does not recognize.

★ ★ ★ ★ ★ ★ ★ ★

Ask the student to draw simple line illustrations of any five of the following: **puppy, cup, porcupine, spot, mop, rope, phone**. The student should then label each drawing and write a sentence telling about each thing. The label word must appear in the sentence. Encourage the student to use as many other **p words** as possible in each sentence. For example: *The pup played on the porch.*

★ ★ ★ ★ ★ ★ ★ ★

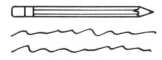

Ask the student to write a paragraph explaining what she/he thinks computers are and how they are used. Encourage the student to use as many **p words** as possible in the paragraph.

From *D'Nealian™ Home/School Activities: Cursive Practice for Grades 4–6*, published by Scott, Foresman and Company.

Ask the student to draw a human figure (stick or realistic) and then draw clothing on the figure. Have the student label all the **o word** clothing by drawing a slanted line from the piece of clothing out to the side and then writing the name of the item at the end of the line. For example, *shoes, socks, coat, bonnet, apron, overalls, shorts*, etc. The student should strive to have at least five such pieces of clothing on the figure.

★ ★ ★ ★ ★ ★ ★ ★

Have the student write the numbers from 1 to 12 in a column on a sheet of paper. Next to each number the student should write one of the following words: **clock, pop, dock, show, rob, odd, lot, gold, goat, roam, poke, zone**. Then ask the student to write a new word for each of the given words by changing just one letter. The **o** must not be changed. For example,

　　　*1. clock　　block (or flock, crock, etc.)*

After the student writes a new word next to each given word, he/she may exchange papers with someone else. Each student should read the other's list of new words aloud.

★ ★ ★ ★ ★ ★ ★ ★

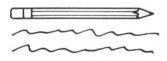

Ask the student to write a story about a cook who tries to cross a brook. Ask the student to use each of the following words at least once in the story: **cook, brook, book, took, crook, shook**.

★ ★ ★ ★ ★ ★ ★ ★

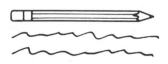

Ask the student to write about a favorite book that she/he has read recently. The student should tell what the story is about and why he/she likes it. When the student finishes, ask her/him to underline all the **o words** in the paragraph(s).

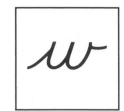

Ask the student to number a sheet of paper from 1 to 10 and write the following words in a column along the left-hand side of the paper: **wall, waste, watch, water, week, wheel, where, whirl, window, wind**. Along the right-hand side the student should write these words in a column: **shield, fall, barrow, pane, dog, end, paper, ever, basket, pool**. Finally, ask the student to create a third list of 10 compound words, each word formed by joining one word from the left-hand column to a word from the right-hand column. For example, *wallpaper, wastebasket*.

★ ★ ★ ★ ★ ★ ★ ★

Ask the student to write a poem that includes each of the following words at least once: **awful, waffle, witch, switch**.

★ ★ ★ ★ ★ ★ ★ ★

Ask the student to write a sentence for each of the following pairs of words:

> **swan/fawn**
> **willow/woods**
> **grow/slow**
> **whale/whopper**
> **wash/watch**

Each sentence must contain both words in the pair. Encourage the student to use as many other **w words** as possible in each sentence. For example: *A fawn watched the swan swim.*

★ ★ ★ ★ ★ ★ ★ ★

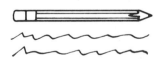

Have the student turn a standard sheet of unlined paper sideways and write across the top in lower-case letters: the winners! Then ask the student to describe a contest and list the names of the first, second, and third prize winners along with the prizes they won. Encourage the student to use as many **w words** as possible. For example: *William Walsh won a watch.*

From *D'Nealian™ Home/School Activities: Cursive Practice for Grades 4–6*, published by Scott, Foresman and Company. Copyright © 1985 Barbara Gregorich.

 Have the student write the numbers from 1 to 6 in a column on a sheet of paper. Next to each number the student should write one of the following words: **bib, double, cub, blubber, fable, rumble**. Then, next to each given word, the student should write a rhyming word. The rhyming word must contain the letter **b**. For example,

*1. bib     rib*

★ ★ ★ ★ ★ ★ ★ ★

 Have the student number two columns from 1 to 10 on a sheet of paper. In the left-hand column the student should write the words pictured in Illustration #2 (1. mice; 2. fire; etc.) on page 36. In the right-hand column the student should write the following adjectives: **black, bashful, bald, broken, blazing, blue, bent, big, busy, beautiful**. Ask the student to write ten sentences, each sentence pairing a word from the left-hand column with an adjective from the right-hand column. For example: *The bald mice bought wigs.*

★ ★ ★ ★ ★ ★ ★ ★

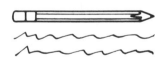 Have the student write a story entitled "Unbelievable World Records" in which the student tells about six different world records set by **Abbie, Elizabeth, Barbara, Abdul, Jacob, Robert**. At least one sentence should be devoted to each record holder. Encourage the student to use at least one other **b word** in each sentence.

★ ★ ★ ★ ★ ★ ★ ★

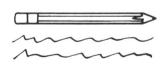 Ask the student to write a story about a buffalo and a bumblebee who become friends and decide to buy some bubblegum. Encourage the student to use as many **b words** as possible in the story.

Ask the student to write a list of at least six singular nouns pictured in Illustration #5 (page 39). Next to each singular noun the student should write the plural form of the noun. For example, *camel     camels.*

Ask the student to write each of the following words on a sheet of paper: **salmon, sari, shark, screwdriver, scissors, snowshoes, shrimp, sickle, sombrero, spatula, suspenders, squid**. Then have the student label three columns across the top of another sheet of paper with the words "Sea Animals," "Tools," and "Clothing." Ask the student to categorize the words on the first sheet by putting them in the appropriate columns on the second sheet. For example,

| *Sea Animals* | *Tools* | *Clothing* |
|---|---|---|
| salmon | sickle | sari |

Encourage the student to use the dictionary for help with unfamiliar words.

Ask the student to select five pictures from newspapers or magazines. The student should then paste each picture on a blank sheet of paper and write a caption below it. At least one word in each caption must contain the letter **s**. Encourage the student to use as many **s words** as possible in the captions.

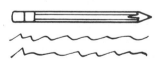
Ask the student to write a short detective story, using at least six of the following words at least once: **sisters, mystery, molasses, silver, soap, task, trash, suds, confess, suspects, missing, treasure**. Encourage the student to use the words in any order he/she wishes and to include as many other **s words** as possible in the story.

 Ask the student to draw a picture of a family eating breakfast together. Then, based on the picture, the student should list all the **r words** that the scene brings to mind. For example, *mother, father, brother, sister, breakfast, cereal, butter,* etc.

 Ask the student to begin a sentence with "A rich rabbit would buy . . ." and then finish the sentence by naming three things. Each item must have an **r** in it. For example, *carrots, celery.*

 Ask the student to write the following pairs of words on a sheet of paper:

**rocking chair/rocking horse**
**rainbow/raincoat**
**rattle/rattlesnake**
**ride/rider**
**reins/reindeer**

Then have the student write a brief explanation of one difference between the two things named in each pair. For example: *My grandfather sits in a rocking chair. My younger brother sits on a rocking horse.*

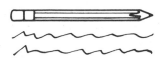 Ask the student to clip a sports story from a newspaper and circle all the **r words** in it. Then have the student write her/his own story about the sport, using as many of the circled **r words** as possible.

From *D'Nealian™ Home/School Activities: Cursive Practice for Grades 4–6*, published by Scott, Foresman and Company. Copyright © 1985 Barbara Gregorich.

Have the student number a sheet of paper from 1 to 5. Next to each number the student should write one of the following names: **Alfred, Cliff, Jeffrey, Steffie, Tiffany.** Ask the student to imagine that she/he has won $1,000 and is going to use some of the money to buy each of these six people a gift. The student should write the name of the gift next to each person's name. For example, *1. Alfred    goldfish.* Each gift must contain the letter **f**, and no two gifts can be identical.

★ ★ ★ ★ ★ ★ ★ ★

Ask the student to write the following words on a piece of paper: **fan, fair, fault, face, faith.** Then ask him/her to write two definitions for each word.

★ ★ ★ ★ ★ ★ ★ ★

Ask the student to write five sentences, each sentence containing one of the following sets of words:

> **giraffe/buffalo/raft**
> **funny/farmer/fat**
> **soft/fawn/fur**
> **fifteen/waffles/awful**
> **finger/face/fell**

For example: *The fur on the fawn was soft.* Encourage the student to use the three words in each set in any order within the sentence.

★ ★ ★ ★ ★ ★ ★ ★

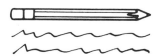

Ask the student to write a description of a milkshake, using each of the following words at least once: **flavor, float, fat, foamy, frosty, full, fudge, freezer, fabulous.** Encourage the student to use the words in any order he/she wishes. When finished writing, the student should exchange papers with someone else, and each student should read the other's description as though it were a radio advertisement.

 Ask the student to label two columns on a sheet of paper, placing the word "Beginning" at the top of one column and the word "Ending" at the top of the other. Under the Beginning heading the student should write as many words as he/she can think of that begin with the letter **z**. For example, *zebra, zero, zip*. Under the Ending heading the student should write as many words as she/he can think of that end with the letter **z**. For example, *quiz, whiz, buzz*. A total of 10 words is good, 15 excellent, 20 outstanding.

★ ★ ★ ★ ★ ★ ★ ★

 Ask the student to write a sentence for each of the following pairs of words:

**zipper/zoo**
**buzzing/zillion**
**squeeze/fuzzy**
**zigzag/zebra**
**amazing/crazy**

Each sentence must contain both words in the pair. For example: *My zipper broke while I was at the zoo.*

★ ★ ★ ★ ★ ★ ★ ★

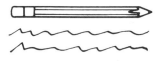 Ask the student to turn a standard sheet of unlined paper sideways and write across the top, in lower-case letters: **zippy zippers**. Then have the student write an ad for zippy zippers, using as many **z words** as possible. When finished writing, the student may exchange ads with someone else, each reading the other's ad aloud.

★ ★ ★ ★ ★ ★ ★ ★

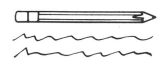 Ask the student to rewrite the story of Goldilocks and the Three Bears as the story of **Crazylocks and the Three Zebras**. Encourage the student to use as many **z words** as possible in the story.

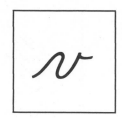

Ask the student to write as many words as he/she can think of that begin with the letter **v**. Then have the student number the words. A list of 10 is good, 15 excellent, 20 outstanding.

★ ★ ★ ★ ★ ★ ★ ★

Ask the student to draw simple line illustrations of any five of the following words: **wave, curve, olive, valentine, valley, vase, vine, volcano, sleeve, cave**. Have the student label each drawing and write a sentence that tells something about it. The label word must appear in each sentence. Encourage the student to use as many other **v words** as possible in each sentence. For example:

> *wave*
> *You must be very brave to jump into a wave.*

★ ★ ★ ★ ★ ★ ★ ★

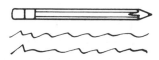

Ask the student to write a story of about seven or eight sentences entitled "The Violent Vacuum Cleaner." Encourage the student to use as many **v words** as possible while describing what might happen if a vacuum cleaner went on a rampage. For example, *it broke a vase, ate a valentine, took the varnish off the floors,* etc.

★ ★ ★ ★ ★ ★ ★ ★

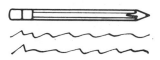

Ask the student to write a personal letter to a friend or family member. The letter must contain at least five of the following words: **very, vitamins, live, give, five, move, even, drive, favorite, volleyball**. Encourage the student to use as many other **v words** as possible in the letter.

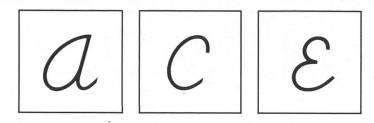

Have the student write "All Aboard" at the top of a sheet of paper. Then ask the student to imagine that she/he is about to take a trip by train. The student should list at least five cities he/she will visit that begin with the letter **A**. For example, *Albany, Anaheim, Albuquerque, Atlanta.*

★ ★ ★ ★ ★ ★ ★ ★

Have the student number a sheet of paper from 1 to 5. Then give the student Illustration #5 (page 39), and ask her/him to write titles for five of the pictures in the illustration. Each title must contain two words that begin with capital **C**. For example, *The Camel by the Cabin.*

★ ★ ★ ★ ★ ★ ★ ★

Have the student number a sheet of paper from 1 to 6. Next to each number the student should write one of the following titles:

**Enough Eggs**
**Eighteen Equal Elephants**
**Eleven Elastic Eels**
**The Empty Envelope**
**The Endless Echo**
**The Emperor's Enemy**

★ ★ ★ ★ ★ ★ ★ ★

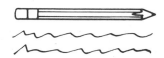

Ask the student to choose one of the titles in the preceding activity and write a story about it. Encourage the student to use as many words beginning with capital **E** as possible in the story.

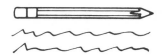

Ask the student to write a story entitled "Olivia Owl and Olga Otter" in which **Olivia Owl** and **Olga Otter** have a contest to see who can make **Ozzie Oyster** open his shell.

★ ★ ★ ★ ★ ★ ★ ★

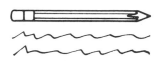

Ask the student to write a story entitled "Hairy Harry's Heavy Hamburgers" in which Harry—who loves hamburgers—starts his own hamburger restaurant. But Hairy Harry's hamburgers turn out to be very heavy. Encourage the student to use as many words beginning with capital **H** as possible, including such words as **He** and **How** to begin sentences.

★ ★ ★ ★ ★ ★ ★ ★

Have the student label three columns across a sheet of paper, placing the word "People" at the top of the first column, "Places" at the top of the second column, and "Things" at the top of the third column. The student should then write as many words beginning with capital **K** as she/he can think of that belong in each column. For example:

| *People* | *Places* | *Things* |
|---|---|---|
| Kevin | Kansas | Kellogg cereals |
| Karen | Kankakee | Kleenex tissues |

A score of 3 words in each category is good, 6 excellent, and 8 outstanding.

★ ★ ★ ★ ★ ★ ★ ★

Have the student write **Mr., Mrs., Miss,** and **Ms.** across the top of a sheet of paper. Then ask the student to number a column on the sheet from 1 to 4. Next to each number the student should write one of the given titles and a proper name. The first and last names of each proper name must begin with **M**, and the middle initial must be **M**. For example, *Mr. Michael M. Maravich; Mrs. Melanie M. Morrison.*

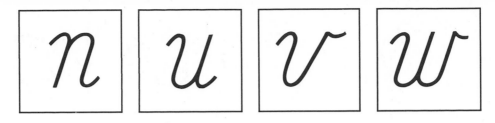

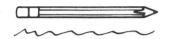 Ask the student to write the following words across a sheet of paper: **Nasty, Nearby, Navy, Natural, Neon, Nearsighted, Ninth, Nice, Noisy, Nylon**. Then give the student Illustration #6 (page 40), and ask her/him to write a three-word title for five of the pictures in the illustration. The middle word of each title must be one of the given words. For example, *A Nasty Squid, The Noisy Queen.*

★ ★ ★ ★ ★ ★ ★ ★

 Show the student Illustration #3 (page 37), and ask him/her to write all the **U words** that the illustration suggests. Each **U word** that the student thinks of must be capitalized. For example, *Unicorn, Umpire, Usher, Umbrella.*

★ ★ ★ ★ ★ ★ ★ ★

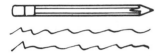 Ask the student to write a story entitled **Victoria's Velvet Vine** in which Victoria grows a very large vine covered with velvet. Encourage the student to use as many words beginning with capital **V** as possible in the story—including, of course, Victoria, who might climb her vine and end up in **Venice** or the land of the **Vikings** or **Vancouver** or any other place that begins with a capital **V**.

★ ★ ★ ★ ★ ★ ★ ★

 Have the student label two columns across a sheet of paper, placing the word "Girls" at the top of one column and "Boys" at the top of the other. Under each column the student should write as many first names as she/he can think of that begin with **W**. For example,

| *Girls* | *Boys* |
|---------|--------|
| Wendy | Walter |
| Wanda | William |
| Wilma | Warren |

From *D'Nealian™ Home/School Activities: Cursive Practice for Grades 4–6*, published by Scott, Foresman and Company. Copyright © 1985 Barbara Gregorich.

Ask the student to number a sheet of paper from 1 to 8. Next to each number the student should write one of the following place names:

> **Youngstown, Ohio**
> **Yorktown, Virginia**
> **Yonkers, New York**
> **Yakima, Washington**
> **Yankton, South Dakota**
> **Yazoo City, Mississippi**
> **Yarmouth, Maine**
> **Yuma, Arizona**

★ ★ ★ ★ ★ ★ ★ ★

Ask the student to write the following words in a column on a sheet of paper: **The, This, That, These, Those**. In another column have the student write the following words: **Tasty, Terrible, Terrific, Tall, Third, Tough, Twelfth, Thin, Top, Tangled**. Then give the student Illustration #2 (page 36), and ask him/her to write a list of ten titles for the pictures in the illustration. Each title must consist of one word from the first column, one word from the second column, and one word appropriate to the picture. For example, *Those Terrible Mice, The Twelfth Fire, These Thin Mittens*. The student may use words from the columns more than once.

★ ★ ★ ★ ★ ★ ★ ★

Ask the student to write a list of words beginning with capital **F**. For example, *Friday, Frisbee, French fries*. A list of 5 is good, 10 excellent, 15 outstanding.

★ ★ ★ ★ ★ ★ ★ ★

Ask the student to write five sentences, each one containing two words that begin with capital **B**. For example: *Barbara visited her cousin who lives in Boston.*

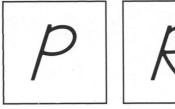 

Ask the student to complete the following sentence with four names that begin with capital **P**: **Pirate Pamela** and **Prince Paul** got married in **Peoria** and named their four children

—————————, —————————, —————————,

and —————————.

★ ★ ★ ★ ★ ★ ★ ★

Ask the student to number a sheet of paper from 1 to 5. Next to each number the student should write the initials **R.R.**, and next to each set of initials the student should write a name having those initials. The names may be real (*Red River, Robert Redford*) or imaginary (*Rudolph Reindeer, Rolling Railroad*).

★ ★ ★ ★ ★ ★ ★ ★

Have the student label two columns across a sheet of paper, placing the word "Girls" at the top of one column and "Boys" at the top of the other. Under each column the student should write as many first names as she/he can think of that begin with capital **G**. For example,

| *Girls* | *Boys* |
|---|---|
| *Gloria* | *George* |
| *Glenda* | *Gabriel* |
| *Gwen* | *Gene* |
| *Gillian* | *Gil* |
| *Gail* | *Greg* |

Have the student number a sheet of paper from 1 to 6. Next to each number the student should write one of the following titles:

**The Silver Snake**            **Seven Sassy Sisters**
**The Swan's Sneakers**         **The Sizzling Steak**
**The Shell's Simple Shape**    **The Sweet-Sounding**
                                **Saxophone**

★ ★ ★ ★ ★ ★ ★ ★

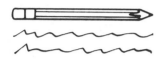

Ask the student to choose one of the titles from the preceding activity and write a story about it. Each story must have at least three characters whose first and last names begin with capital **S**. For example, *Samantha Shell, Steven Swan, Sam Smith*, etc.

★ ★ ★ ★ ★ ★ ★ ★

Ask the student to number a sheet of paper from 1 to 7. Next to each number the student should write one of the following place names:

**Idaho Falls, Idaho**         **Indianapolis, Indiana**
**Indian Valley, Idaho**       **Independence, Iowa**
**Island Lake, Illinois**      **Iowa City, Iowa**
**Indian Heights, Indiana**

★ ★ ★ ★ ★ ★ ★ ★

Ask the student to choose one of the following pairs of names and write a sentence about the characters:

**Zack/Zebulon**
**Zenobia/Zoe**
**Zane/Zelda**
**Zeke/Zeno**

For example: *Did you know that Zack and Zebulon are twins?*

★ ★ ★ ★ ★ ★ ★ ★

Ask the student to write the following words across a sheet of paper: **Queen, Quilt, Quiet, Quick, Quacking, Quarter, Questions, Quiz, Quadruplets, Quarrel, Quicksand**. Then have the student make up the names of three television shows using forms of these capital **Q words**. For example, *The Quiet Queen's Questions, Quilting Quiz, Quarreling Quadruplets*, etc.

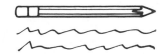

Ask the student to write the following names in a column: **Isadora Duncan; W.E.B. Du Bois; Dorothea Dix; Bob Dylan**. Then have the student look up these people in an encyclopedia and write one or more sentences about each famous person. The student must use the person's name in at least one of the sentences.

★ ★ ★ ★ ★ ★ ★ ★

Ask the student to number a sheet of paper from 1 to 5. Next to each number the student should write a proper name consisting of both a first name and last name. All the first names must begin with **J**, and no two first names may be identical. All the last names must also begin with **J**, and no last name may be used more than twice. For example, *Jennifer Johnson, Jeremy Johnson, Joel Jarman, Janet Jarzynski*, etc.

★ ★ ★ ★ ★ ★ ★ ★

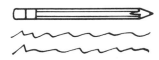

Ask the student to write a short paragraph entitled "The X-Ray Machine." In the paragraph the student should describe both the benefits and the potential dangers of X-ray machines. Encourage the student to find the needed information in an encyclopedia.

★ ★ ★ ★ ★ ★ ★ ★

Ask the student to write five sentences, each one containing two proper names that begin with capital **L**. For example: *Larry read a poem about Abraham Lincoln.*

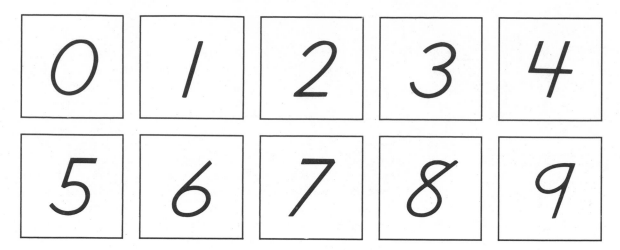

Have the student number a sheet of paper from 1 to 5. Next to each number the student should list favorite foods in order of preference. Then ask the student to do the same thing for rock stars, television programs, and animals, numbering each of the lists.

★ ★ ★ ★ ★ ★ ★ ★

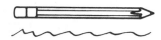

Have the student write the following names on a sheet of paper: Baker Street, Fifth Avenue, Michigan Boulevard, Pine Circle, Jaspar Lane. Then ask the student to write five sentences, each one containing the name of one of the streets and a 3- or 4-digit street number. For example: *Nora delivered the package to 423 Baker Street.*

★ ★ ★ ★ ★ ★ ★ ★

Ask the student to write five slogans such as those that appear on T-shirts, bumper stickers, and posters. Each slogan must contain a numeral and a word that rhymes with it. For example: *4 is a bore. 7 is heaven. We dine at 9.*

★ ★ ★ ★ ★ ★ ★ ★

Ask the student to number a sheet of paper from 1 to 4. Beside each number the student should write one of the following numerals: **66, 77, 88, 99**. Then, next to each numeral, the student should write a word or phrase that—when said with the numeral— is alliterative (repeats the beginning sound). For example, *66 silly silkworms, 88 aching apes.*

*Illustration #1* • 35

*Illustration #3 • 37*

*Illustration #5* • *39*

squid          quilt
quicksand      equal
square         queen
earthquake     quarrel
squirrel       question mark